Starting a Social Media Management Business Using AI

Your Step-by-Step Blueprint

Launch and Scale a Profitable SMM Venture Effortlessly with Artificial Intelligence

Alejandro S. Diego

Table of Contents

Introduction

In recent years, artificial intelligence has transitioned from being a futuristic concept to a present-day powerhouse, transforming industries across the globe. Among the areas most impacted by this technological revolution is social media management. The sheer volume of content, engagement metrics, and the fast pace at which social platforms evolve makes it difficult for businesses to keep up manually. AI steps in to simplify, optimize, and scale these efforts, giving businesses a much-needed edge. From automating repetitive tasks like post scheduling to analyzing vast datasets to predict audience preferences, AI reshapes the way social media is managed, allowing companies to achieve more with fewer resources.

Social media platforms are where consumers spend a significant portion of their time, making them crucial for businesses aiming to connect with their audiences. However, managing multiple platforms while ensuring consistent, high-quality engagement can be overwhelming. AI changes the game by offering tools that automate content creation, scheduling, and real-time engagement monitoring. This shift allows businesses to reach a larger audience, personalize their interactions, and optimize their strategies, all while saving time and effort. It's no longer just about being on social media—it's about using technology to be strategic, efficient, and impactful.

The idea of starting a social media management business powered by AI presents a unique, profitable opportunity. As businesses increasingly recognize the value of maintaining a strong online presence, the demand for social media managers continues to grow. Yet, many business owners don't have the time or expertise to manage their social channels effectively. This is where an AI-driven approach shines. By automating much of the work traditionally done manually, AI empowers you to handle multiple clients effortlessly, providing them with top-tier service at a fraction of the usual time and cost. The efficiency AI offers means you can scale your business quickly, taking on more clients without burning out or needing a large team.

The goal of this book is simple: to show you how to leverage AI to launch and grow your own social media management business. Whether you're just starting or looking to take your existing business to the next level, this guide will provide you with the tools and strategies necessary to succeed. By the end of this book, you'll have a clear understanding of how to use AI to automate tasks, improve client results, and scale your business—opening up new possibilities for income and growth. AI is not just a trend; it's a tool that, when used correctly, can lead to long-term success in the ever-evolving world of social media management.

Chapter 1: Understanding Artificial Intelligence and Social Media

Artificial Intelligence, commonly known as AI, refers to the simulation of human intelligence by machines, particularly computer systems. It encompasses a broad range of capabilities, including learning, reasoning, problem-solving, understanding language, and even visual perception. Unlike traditional software programs that follow predefined rules, AI systems can analyze data, learn from patterns, and make decisions autonomously. The evolution of AI has been rapid, driven by advancements in computing power, access to massive amounts of data, and breakthroughs in machine learning algorithms. Over time, AI has shifted from being an abstract concept explored in labs to becoming an integral part of everyday life, powering everything from virtual assistants to autonomous vehicles.

The roots of AI can be traced back to the 1950s, when researchers first started exploring the possibility of creating machines that could "think" like humans. Early AI systems were limited in scope and capability, but as technology advanced, so did AI's potential. Machine learning—a subset of AI that enables systems to learn and improve from experience without being explicitly programmed—has been a major driver of AI's progress. Today, deep learning, which involves training AI models with vast amounts of data, allows machines to recognize speech, detect patterns, and even generate creative content. The continuous improvement in AI's ability to process and understand complex information is what makes it so valuable across industries.

In the realm of social media, AI has proven to be a transformative force. Social platforms generate an immense volume of data daily, from user interactions to content uploads and engagement metrics. For businesses and marketers, manually analyzing and responding to this data in real-time is impractical. AI steps in by automating much of this workload. It can analyze user behavior to predict trends, suggest optimal posting times, and even generate content based on what's most likely to resonate with a target audience. For example, AI can sift through thousands of comments to identify customer sentiment, flag potential PR crises, or recommend how brands should engage with their audience in a more personalized manner.

Beyond analytics, AI is revolutionizing content creation. Tools that use AI to write social media posts, create visual content, and even design ad campaigns are becoming indispensable for businesses looking to maintain a strong online presence. AI can quickly adapt to trends, monitor performance, and adjust strategies accordingly, allowing businesses to stay relevant in an increasingly competitive space. By leveraging AI, companies can efficiently manage multiple social media channels, customize their approach for different audiences, and ensure that their message is delivered with precision and consistency.

The social media landscape has evolved from a place of casual interaction to a sophisticated marketing and engagement platform. AI plays a pivotal role in this evolution, offering solutions that not only automate but also enhance the way brands communicate with their audience. From personalized recommendations to predictive algorithms, AI is pushing the boundaries of what's possible in social media management, making it easier for businesses to connect with their audience in more meaningful and impactful ways.

The advantages of incorporating AI into social media management are vast and game-changing for businesses of all sizes. AI not only streamlines repetitive tasks but also introduces new capabilities that were previously unattainable through manual efforts. One of the primary benefits is automation. Social media management often requires posting content at optimal times, engaging with audiences, and monitoring activity across multiple platforms. With AI, much of this can be automated.

Scheduling posts, responding to comments, and even generating reports can be done without constant human intervention. This frees up valuable time for businesses to focus on strategic planning rather than getting bogged down in day-to-day operations.

Another significant advantage is AI's ability to assist with content creation. Tools powered by AI can generate engaging copy for posts, suggest trending topics, and even create eye-catching visuals. These tools analyze data from millions of social media interactions to understand what types of content are most likely to resonate with audiences. For example, AI can help craft personalized messages for different segments of a brand's audience, ensuring that each post feels relevant and timely. This not only increases engagement but also helps brands build deeper relationships with their followers.

Engagement analytics is another area where AI excels. Social media platforms generate enormous amounts of data, from likes and shares to comments and click-through rates. Manually analyzing this data is time-consuming and often ineffective due to the complexity of human behavior online. AI, however, can quickly sift through these vast datasets to uncover insights. It can identify patterns in user behavior, predict which types of content will perform best, and even suggest ways to improve future engagement. For brands, this means they can fine-tune their social media strategies based on real-time data, making more informed decisions that lead to better results.

AI can also provide real-time responses to users. Through AI-powered chatbots, businesses can engage with customers 24/7, answering questions, providing recommendations, and handling customer service inquiries instantly. This level of responsiveness helps maintain high levels of customer satisfaction and ensures that no opportunities for engagement are missed. Additionally, AI can personalize these interactions, making customers feel like they're receiving individualized attention even in automated exchanges.

Several businesses have already embraced AI in their social media strategies and seen significant success. One such example is Netflix, which uses AI to personalize its social media interactions and suggest content tailored to individual preferences. By leveraging AI algorithms that predict what users want to watch based on their viewing habits, Netflix ensures its posts and advertisements are always relevant to the audience, boosting engagement and encouraging users to spend more time on the platform.

Coca-Cola is another brand that has capitalized on AI for its social media campaigns. The company uses AI to monitor consumer sentiment on social media platforms, tracking mentions of its products and gathering insights into how people feel about the brand. By understanding these sentiments, Coca-Cola can adjust its marketing strategies in real time, making sure it stays aligned with customer expectations. This level of responsiveness helps the company maintain a positive image and quickly address any potential issues before they escalate.

Sephora, a global beauty retailer, has also integrated AI into its social media presence. Sephora uses AI to engage with customers through chatbots that offer personalized product recommendations. These AI-driven interactions are not only efficient but also highly tailored to each user's preferences, creating a more engaging shopping experience. By automating customer service and providing personalized responses, Sephora keeps its audience engaged while driving sales through social platforms.

These examples highlight the enormous potential of AI in social media management. Whether it's automating content creation, improving engagement analytics, or personalizing interactions, AI enables businesses to work smarter, scale faster, and connect with audiences in more meaningful ways. By incorporating AI into their social media strategies, companies are not just keeping up with the competition—they're staying ahead of the curve.

Chapter 2: Essential AI Tools for Social Media Management

In today's digital landscape, businesses have access to a wide range of powerful AI tools that simplify and enhance social media management. These tools are designed to handle various aspects of social media, from post scheduling and content creation to engagement tracking and managing multiple clients. By leveraging these technologies, businesses can automate tasks, optimize performance, and achieve more in less time. Here's an overview of some of the most effective AI-driven tools available today.

For post scheduling, AI platforms like **Buffer**, **Hootsuite**, and **Later** have revolutionized the way businesses manage their social media timelines. These tools allow users to automate the posting process by scheduling content to be published at optimal times based on audience activity. Buffer, for instance, provides insights into when your audience is most active, helping you schedule posts for maximum reach and engagement. Hootsuite, a comprehensive social media management platform, goes beyond scheduling, offering analytics, monitoring, and team collaboration features. Later, which focuses heavily on visual platforms like Instagram and Pinterest, allows users to visually plan their content and automate posts, making it perfect for brands that rely on imagery to connect with their audience. These tools streamline the process of maintaining a consistent presence across multiple social media platforms without the need for constant manual intervention.

When it comes to content creation, tools like **ChatGPT**, **Jasper.ai**, and **Canva** are leading the charge in automating creativity. **ChatGPT**, an AI language model developed by OpenAI, can generate engaging and human-like text for social media posts, blog articles, and other types of content. It's especially useful for businesses that need to produce large volumes of content quickly. **Jasper.ai**, another AI writing tool, excels at generating marketing copy, social media captions, and even full blog posts. Jasper can be tailored to match your brand's voice, helping ensure consistency in tone across all content. For visual content, **Canva** integrates AI to assist users in designing professional-quality graphics without the need for extensive design experience. Canva's AI-powered suggestions help businesses create on-brand visuals that resonate with their audience, making it easier to produce high-quality content in a fraction of the time.

Engagement tracking is another area where AI shines. Tools like **Sprout Social**, **Socialbakers**, and **Brandwatch** help businesses monitor their audience's interactions, track performance, and derive actionable insights. **Sprout Social** provides comprehensive analytics and engagement tools, allowing businesses to track their social media performance in real time. With AI-powered reporting, Sprout offers recommendations for optimizing content, improving engagement, and identifying key influencers within your audience. **Socialbakers** leverages AI to provide in-depth analysis of audience demographics, behaviors, and preferences, helping businesses fine-tune their strategies. **Brandwatch** goes even further, using AI to track brand mentions, analyze consumer sentiment, and monitor trends across various social platforms. These tools not only make engagement tracking more efficient but also provide a deeper understanding of what drives interactions, enabling businesses to adjust their approach and connect with their audience in more meaningful ways.

Managing multiple clients can be a daunting task, but AI-powered platforms like **Zoho Social** and **Agorapulse** make it significantly easier. **Zoho Social** is designed for agencies and businesses that manage multiple social media accounts for different clients. It offers robust features for scheduling, monitoring, and reporting, allowing users to manage several accounts from a single dashboard. Zoho Social also includes AI-driven features like smart queues, which automatically schedule posts based on audience activity, ensuring content is posted at the best times. **Agorapulse** similarly provides a unified platform for managing multiple clients. It offers advanced scheduling tools, social listening capabilities, and detailed reporting features that help businesses stay organized while delivering top-tier service to their clients. With AI-enhanced automation, both Zoho Social and Agorapulse allow social media managers to handle more clients without compromising the quality of their services.

These AI-powered tools collectively transform the way businesses approach social media management. By automating tasks like scheduling, content creation, engagement tracking, and client management, these platforms allow businesses to scale their efforts efficiently and focus on what truly matters—building meaningful connections with their audience and driving results. Whether you're a freelancer managing a few accounts or an agency handling dozens of clients, these tools empower you to optimize your workflow, improve performance, and ultimately grow your business.

Choosing the right AI tools for your social media management business is a critical step in building an efficient and scalable operation. With so many options available, it's important to follow a structured approach to ensure that you select tools that align with your business goals and the specific needs of your clients. Here's a step-by-step guide to help you navigate this process:

Step 1: Define Your Business Needs

Before diving into AI tools, start by identifying the specific tasks you want to automate or optimize. Are you looking to streamline post scheduling, improve content creation, or enhance engagement tracking? Perhaps you need a tool to manage multiple clients efficiently. Knowing your core needs will help you focus on tools that offer the features you actually require, rather than getting distracted by unnecessary extras.

For instance, if you run a small agency with several clients, managing their accounts simultaneously may be your primary challenge. In that case, a comprehensive tool like **Zoho Social** or **Agorapulse** would be ideal for managing multiple accounts in one place. If content creation is your bottleneck, tools like **ChatGPT** or **Canva** may be more relevant.

Step 2: Research Available Tools

Once you have a clear understanding of your needs, start researching tools that meet those criteria. Look for AI platforms that specialize in the areas you want to enhance. Compare features, pricing plans, and user reviews to get a sense of which tools are the best fit for your business. Keep scalability in mind—ensure that the tools you choose can grow with your business as you take on more clients or expand your service offerings.

For example, if you're starting out and need an affordable solution for scheduling posts, **Later** or **Buffer** may be suitable. As you grow, you might need more robust analytics and client management features, in which case **Sprout Social** or **Hootsuite** could be better long-term solutions.

Step 3: Test Tools with Free Trials

Many AI tools offer free trials or demo versions. Take advantage of these opportunities to test the platforms before making a commitment. During your trial period, explore how the tool integrates into your workflow, its ease of use, and whether it genuinely improves your efficiency. Consider how intuitive the interface is, how much time it saves you, and whether it delivers the promised results. Testing tools firsthand is crucial to understanding whether they'll work for your business in the long term.

For instance, if you're testing **Jasper.ai** for content creation, create a few posts and evaluate the quality and relevance of the AI-generated content. If you're using **Sprout Social** for engagement tracking, check how well it presents analytics and whether the insights it provides align with your business goals.

Step 4: Evaluate Integration Capabilities

The AI tools you choose should integrate seamlessly with your existing systems, such as your CRM, email marketing software, or other business management tools. Check whether the platform offers API integrations with the tools you're already using. Efficient integration helps maintain a smooth workflow and reduces the time spent manually transferring data between systems.

For example, if you're using **Zoho CRM** to manage client relationships, choosing **Zoho Social** would be advantageous since both platforms integrate seamlessly. Similarly, if you're using **Canva** to create visuals, ensure that your social media scheduling tool, like **Later**, integrates easily for a streamlined process.

Step 5: Analyze Costs and Return on Investment (ROI)

While some AI tools come with significant upfront costs, it's important to weigh those costs against the potential ROI. Calculate how much time and effort the tool will save you and how it will improve your business's efficiency and client satisfaction. Some tools might be more expensive initially, but if they help you scale your business by handling more clients or producing better results, they're likely worth the investment.

For example, **Hootsuite** may seem costly compared to basic scheduling tools, but if its analytics and team collaboration features allow you to offer higher-quality services, it may provide better long-term value for your business.

Step 6: Monitor and Adjust

After selecting and implementing your AI tools, it's important to continuously monitor their performance. Evaluate whether the tool is delivering the expected results and improving your efficiency. If you find that certain tools aren't as effective as anticipated, don't hesitate to switch to alternatives that better suit your evolving needs. AI tools are constantly improving, and staying flexible allows you to take advantage of new technologies as they emerge.

Businesses Successfully Using AI Tools

1. Netflix: Personalizing Social Media Content Netflix has become a master at using AI to engage its audience across social media platforms. By utilizing AI algorithms, Netflix customizes its content recommendations for users, ensuring that the content posted on its social channels is highly relevant. Netflix analyzes user behavior data to predict what content will resonate most with specific segments of its audience. This targeted approach drives higher engagement rates and keeps users interacting with their brand across multiple platforms.

By leveraging AI-driven insights, Netflix has been able to refine its content strategies to engage more effectively, boosting not only viewership but also their brand's influence on social media.

2. Coca-Cola: Monitoring Sentiment in Real-Time Coca-Cola uses AI to monitor social media conversations and gauge consumer sentiment in real time. With tools like **Brandwatch**, Coca-Cola is able to track mentions of its brand and products, analyze how consumers feel about the brand, and respond quickly to any negative sentiment. By acting on this AI-driven analysis, Coca-Cola can adjust its marketing campaigns and customer outreach strategies to ensure that it remains aligned with consumer expectations and preferences.

The ability to track sentiment in real time has allowed Coca-Cola to maintain a positive brand image, respond swiftly to potential PR crises, and engage customers more meaningfully.

3. Sephora: AI-Powered Customer Engagement Sephora has integrated AI-powered chatbots into its social media platforms, using them to engage customers in real time. These chatbots, powered by tools like **Sprout Social**, offer personalized product recommendations based on a user's preferences, previous purchases, and beauty goals. This level of personalization has increased customer satisfaction and boosted sales through social media channels.

By automating customer interactions and personalizing the shopping experience, Sephora has been able to scale its customer service efforts while maintaining high engagement across its social platforms.

4. HubSpot: Streamlining Social Media Campaigns HubSpot uses AI tools like **Hootsuite** to manage its social media presence across multiple channels. By leveraging AI for scheduling and engagement analytics, HubSpot has been able to streamline its social media campaigns, ensuring that content is posted at optimal times and audience engagement is maximized. HubSpot's use of AI for performance tracking allows the company to continuously refine its social media strategy, leading to improved ROI from their campaigns.

The combination of automation and analytics has enabled HubSpot to maintain a strong social media presence without dedicating excessive resources to manual tasks, allowing the company to focus more on strategy and creative content.

These case studies highlight the real-world impact of AI on social media management. Whether it's personalizing content, monitoring sentiment, or improving engagement tracking, these companies demonstrate how AI tools can enhance a brand's social media efforts, leading to increased efficiency, better customer experiences, and greater overall success.

Chapter 3: Setting Up Your AI-Powered Social Media Management Business

Building a successful social media management (SMM) business requires a solid foundation and a clear strategy from the start. The blueprint for creating this foundation begins with thoughtful planning, strategic decision-making, and selecting the right tools and models that align with your goals. Here's a step-by-step guide to establishing the base for your SMM business and choosing a business model that fits your vision.

The first step in creating your SMM business is to define your niche and target audience. Social media management is a broad field, and narrowing your focus allows you to specialize and stand out. Whether you focus on specific industries like fashion, tech, or hospitality, or cater to a particular type of client, such as small businesses or influencers, specialization helps you create tailored services that resonate with your audience. Research potential clients, understand their needs, and identify how your services can solve their problems.

Next, you need to decide what services you'll offer. An SMM business can include a wide range of services, from post scheduling and content creation to analytics, strategy development, and paid advertising management. Offering a combination of these services allows you to provide comprehensive solutions, but it's important to balance what you offer with your capabilities and resources. As an AI-driven SMM business, leveraging AI tools to automate time-consuming tasks like content scheduling and analytics can help you offer more without needing a large team.

Once you have a clear understanding of your niche and service offerings, it's time to choose the business model that will guide your operations. There are three main models to consider: freelance, agency, and consultancy.

1. Freelance Model The freelance model is ideal for individuals looking to offer SMM services independently. This model provides maximum flexibility, allowing you to set your own schedule and take on as many or as few clients as you wish. Freelancers typically work with small businesses, entrepreneurs, or influencers who need hands-on, personalized social media support. With the rise of AI tools, freelancers can manage multiple clients simultaneously by automating many of the manual tasks associated with social media management.

In this model, you'll likely be responsible for all aspects of the business, from client acquisition to execution. Freelancers usually offer a range of packages or hourly services, depending on the client's needs and budget. AI tools will be your biggest asset in this model, as they allow you to manage time efficiently, handle multiple platforms for different clients, and deliver results without burning out.

The freelance model works well if you prefer autonomy and want to keep your operation lean, with minimal overhead costs. It's also a great option for those just starting out, as it allows you to test the market and gradually scale up without significant upfront investment.

2. Agency Model The agency model is designed for those who envision managing a team and scaling their operations to handle multiple clients at a larger scale. An SMM agency typically offers a full suite of social media services, including strategy development, content creation, scheduling, engagement tracking, analytics, and paid advertising. With an agency, you can take on a wider range of clients, from small businesses to large corporations, and charge higher fees due to the comprehensive nature of your services.

One of the advantages of running an agency is that you can hire specialists for different tasks, such as content creators, social media strategists, or ad managers, allowing you to provide top-tier services across the board. AI tools become even more essential in this model, as they enable your team to collaborate efficiently, manage multiple client accounts, and automate repetitive tasks, freeing up time for strategy and client relationships.

The agency model typically involves more complex workflows, but it offers greater potential for scalability and revenue generation. However, it does come with higher operational costs, as you'll need to invest in technology, marketing, and possibly office space as your business grows. If you're looking to build a larger, more structured business with long-term growth potential, the agency model might be the best fit.

3. Consultancy Model The consultancy model focuses on providing high-level strategic advice rather than executing day-to-day social media tasks. Consultants are often brought in by businesses that need expert guidance on how to optimize their social media presence, develop a long-term strategy, or launch new campaigns. This model is less about managing client accounts and more about offering deep expertise, strategic direction, and insights on trends, tools, and best practices.

As a social media consultant, you might offer services such as social media audits, strategy development, performance evaluations, and training for in-house teams. AI tools play a crucial role in this model by providing the data and insights needed to craft effective strategies. AI-driven analytics platforms like **Brandwatch** or **Sprout Social** allow you to present clients with detailed reports on their social media performance, competitor analysis, and audience engagement trends.

The consultancy model is ideal if you have a strong background in social media and enjoy working in an advisory capacity rather than handling the execution of campaigns. It's also a good option if you want to work with a smaller number of high-paying clients, offering them your expertise in a more targeted, strategic way.

In summary, selecting the right business model for your SMM business depends on your goals, expertise, and how you want to structure your operations. If you prefer flexibility and independence, the freelance model is a great starting point, especially with AI tools to support your workflow. For those who want to scale their operations and build a larger team, the agency model offers the best potential for growth and profitability. If you're more interested in providing strategic guidance and working with high-level clients, the consultancy model could be the perfect fit.

No matter which model you choose, AI will be your key ally in optimizing your processes, delivering results, and growing your business efficiently. As you continue to build your SMM business, AI tools will empower you to provide more value to clients while saving time and resources, ultimately positioning you for long-term success.

To build a streamlined and scalable social media management business, setting up AI systems for maximum efficiency is crucial. This not only helps you manage day-to-day tasks with ease but also ensures that your business runs smoothly, allowing you to focus on growth and strategy. The right AI systems will enable you to automate repetitive tasks, keep client relationships organized, and maintain a professional online presence, all while ensuring that your legal structure is sound for long-term success.

Automating post scheduling is one of the most significant time-savers in a social media management business. Instead of manually uploading content for each client daily, AI-powered tools like Buffer, Hootsuite, or Later allow you to schedule posts across multiple platforms in advance. These tools can help identify the best times to post based on audience activity, ensuring that your content is published when engagement is highest. By utilizing AI to automate this process, you can effectively manage the social media accounts of multiple clients without the need to constantly monitor each one, freeing up your time for more strategic tasks. Additionally, with AI tools analyzing performance in real-time, adjustments can be made quickly, keeping content strategies agile and effective.

Automating client workflows is another key element of efficiency. From onboarding new clients to managing ongoing projects, AI tools can help you streamline communication and task management. For example, platforms like Zapier or Asana can automate repetitive actions, such as sending welcome emails, assigning tasks, or generating client reports. By setting up automated workflows, you reduce the margin for human error and ensure that every step of the client process—from initial contact to delivery—is handled with precision and consistency. This level of automation not only enhances client satisfaction but also enables you to take on more clients without feeling overwhelmed by administrative tasks.

Another essential component of maximizing efficiency is centralizing client management using AI-powered CRM systems. Tools like Zoho CRM or HubSpot offer comprehensive solutions to keep track of client information, project timelines, and communication history. These platforms allow you to manage all your clients from one central hub, making it easier to maintain relationships and ensure that nothing slips through the cracks. With AI-driven CRMs, you can also track client engagement, identify trends, and make data-driven decisions that help improve the services you offer. This level of organization and insight ensures that your business runs smoothly, no matter how many clients you are managing at once.

While setting up your AI systems is vital for operational efficiency, building your brand and online presence is equally important for attracting clients and establishing credibility. Potential clients will look at how well you manage your own social media profiles as a reflection of your expertise. Start by creating a professional website that clearly outlines your services, client success stories, and the value you provide. Use social media channels like LinkedIn, Instagram, or Twitter to showcase your knowledge of the industry, share case studies, and provide valuable tips to your audience. By doing so, you not only attract new clients but also build trust in your capabilities as a social media manager who uses AI effectively to drive results.

Additionally, use AI tools to optimize your online presence. AI-powered design platforms like Canva can help you create eye-catching visuals for your website and social media. Chatbots can also be integrated into your website, offering 24/7 support for prospective clients and ensuring that no opportunity for engagement is missed. By leveraging AI for your own brand, you demonstrate the potential of these tools, making a compelling case for prospective clients who are looking for efficient and innovative social media management solutions.

As your business grows, it's important to ensure that you are legally structured for long-term success. The first step is choosing the right business entity, whether it's a sole proprietorship, LLC, or corporation. Each structure comes with its own legal and tax implications, so it's wise to consult with an accountant or legal advisor to determine what's best for your business model and future goals. An LLC, for example, offers flexibility in taxation and protects your personal assets from business liabilities, making it a popular choice for many small business owners.

Alongside structuring your business, it's essential to have well-drafted contracts that outline the scope of work, payment terms, and any deliverables for your clients. These contracts should include clauses for confidentiality, intellectual property rights, and cancellation policies to protect both you and your clients. Legal templates can be customized to fit the specific needs of your social media management business, and tools like Dubsado or HelloSign can automate the client onboarding process, making it easy for both parties to sign and store contracts digitally.

Lastly, don't overlook the importance of proper tax planning and compliance. Depending on your location and the legal structure you choose, you may need to pay self-employment taxes, file quarterly tax estimates, or register for VAT or sales tax. Using accounting software like QuickBooks or Xero can help you stay on top of your finances, track expenses, and ensure that you're prepared come tax season. Setting aside a portion of your income for taxes will save you from any surprises down the road, and working with an accountant ensures that you're taking advantage of any deductions available to your business.

Having a solid legal foundation also means creating terms of service and privacy policies for your website. As a social media manager, you'll likely be handling sensitive client data, and these legal documents will clarify how you protect that information. Data privacy regulations, such as GDPR, apply to businesses handling personal data, so it's important to stay informed about legal obligations to protect both your business and your clients.

By setting up AI systems for automation, centralizing your client management, building a strong brand, and ensuring your business is legally sound, you'll create a scalable and efficient social media management business. These foundational elements will allow you to grow confidently, offering high-quality services to your clients while optimizing your operations with the power of AI.

Chapter 4: Creating Content with AI: Tips and Best Practices

Artificial intelligence has revolutionized the process of generating engaging and high-quality content, making it easier for social media managers to produce relevant material that resonates with their audience. One of the most significant ways AI assists in this area is through its ability to analyze vast amounts of data to understand trends, audience behavior, and the kind of content that is most likely to succeed. By processing this data, AI can suggest topics, formats, and even tones that will engage your target audience, ensuring your content feels relevant, timely, and personalized.

AI-powered tools such as ChatGPT or Jasper.ai are game-changers for generating written content. These platforms are designed to create social media captions, blog posts, and even longer articles with minimal input. You can provide these tools with a prompt or a few key points, and they will generate text that is both coherent and engaging. The advantage of using AI for content generation is that it saves a significant amount of time while still producing content that is aligned with your brand's voice. Additionally, AI tools learn from previous data, meaning they can generate increasingly refined and customized content the more they are used. This allows businesses to maintain a consistent posting schedule without the stress of coming up with fresh ideas manually.

When it comes to creating visuals, AI tools like Canva have become indispensable for social media managers. Canva's AI-driven design suggestions make it easy to create professional-quality graphics, even without a background in design. By analyzing design trends and the type of visuals that work best on different platforms, Canva's AI can recommend layouts, fonts, and color schemes that not only look appealing but are also optimized for audience engagement. This allows you to quickly generate high-quality graphics for Instagram posts,

Facebook ads, or Twitter banners that catch attention and enhance brand recognition.

AI can also help create visuals that are tailored to specific audiences. For example, it can analyze the demographics and preferences of your target group and suggest designs that are more likely to appeal to them, whether that involves using certain color palettes, imagery, or even text placement. This level of customization is key to ensuring that your visual content connects with your audience on a deeper level, making it more likely to be shared, liked, and commented on.

Another important function AI offers in content creation is in writing captions. Crafting the perfect caption for social media posts often involves striking a balance between being informative and engaging, while also maintaining brevity. AI tools can analyze the performance of previous posts to understand which types of captions performed best—whether they were longer and descriptive, or short and punchy. Based on this analysis, AI can then generate captions that match your audience's preferences, using the right keywords and tone to maximize engagement. These tools can even help A/B test different caption options, providing insights into which version resonates better with your audience and boosting your chances of increasing interactions.

In the case of blog posts, AI tools like Jasper.ai can generate longer, well-structured content that matches your brand's tone and style. You can feed the AI a topic, and it will generate a complete blog post with an introduction, body, and conclusion. This helps you maintain a consistent publishing schedule, which is crucial for keeping your audience engaged over time. AI's ability to quickly produce blog content also means you can cover more topics in less time, allowing you to respond to trends or news in your industry more efficiently. This is particularly useful for businesses that want to stay ahead of the curve and consistently produce fresh, relevant content without overwhelming their in-house teams.

Using AI to optimize content creation also reduces the guesswork involved in crafting posts that perform well. Many AI content tools are equipped with SEO capabilities, meaning they can suggest keywords, phrases, and structures that are more likely to rank highly in search results. This helps ensure that your content reaches a broader audience, driving more traffic to your blog, website, or social media channels. Additionally, by using AI-generated data on which keywords or topics are trending, you can position your content to be part of timely conversations, increasing its chances of being discovered and shared.

The beauty of AI in content creation is that it not only automates the process but also enhances the quality of the output. By leveraging data and advanced algorithms, AI tools can produce content that is more targeted, visually appealing, and strategically aligned with your audience's preferences. Whether you're creating quick social media captions, in-depth blog posts, or eye-catching visuals, AI gives you the edge to produce high-quality content with minimal effort, allowing you to focus on broader strategic tasks and client relationships. The result is a more efficient content creation process, more engaging posts, and ultimately, better results for your social media management business.

While AI-generated content is a powerful tool for social media management, balancing it with human creativity and a personal touch is essential for ensuring that the content remains authentic and engaging. AI excels at handling repetitive tasks, generating ideas, and analyzing data, but it lacks the nuanced understanding of context, emotion, and originality that human creativity brings to the table. By combining the efficiency of AI with the personal insights and creativity that only humans can provide, you can create content that is both highly effective and emotionally resonant with your audience.

AI-generated content, such as captions, blog posts, and visual elements, often follows patterns based on past data. It can suggest trending topics, optimize content for engagement, and even write entire pieces. However, to ensure that your content doesn't feel too generic or robotic, it's important to add a personal layer to the AI-generated output. This can be as simple as injecting humor, adjusting the tone to better reflect your brand's voice, or adding personal anecdotes or insights that AI cannot replicate. By doing this, you maintain a unique brand personality that resonates with your audience and differentiates your content from the flood of AI-generated material online.

Human creativity is particularly crucial when developing content that evokes emotions, builds connections, or addresses sensitive topics. AI can suggest words and images based on trends, but it cannot fully grasp the emotional subtleties that drive audience engagement. For example, when creating a campaign around a social cause or a holiday season, a purely AI-generated approach might lack the empathy or cultural context necessary to make the message truly impactful. By adding your own experiences, understanding, and emotional intelligence into the content, you create posts that are not only engaging but also deeply meaningful to your audience.

Ensuring originality is another important aspect when using AI for content creation. AI tools are great at pulling from existing data, but this can sometimes result in content that feels repetitive or formulaic. To avoid this, it's essential to use AI as a foundation or starting point rather than the entire creative process. For example, you can use AI to draft an outline or suggest ideas but then refine, expand, and personalize the content manually to make sure it's truly original. This approach not only keeps your content fresh but also prevents over-reliance on AI-generated material, which could diminish the uniqueness of your brand voice.

Another way to ensure originality is by maintaining a hands-on approach to the final editing process. Even if AI generates an entire blog post or social media caption, taking the time to review and tweak the content allows you to infuse it with your unique perspective. Adding personal reflections, adjusting the phrasing, or incorporating relevant industry insights will help your content stand out from other AI-assisted posts that might lack these elements. This human touch ensures that your brand remains distinctive, relevant, and memorable.

Over-reliance on AI can lead to a loss of creativity and personalization, which are essential for building strong connections with your audience. While AI-generated content can help with efficiency, the most successful brands are those that balance technology with human input. AI should enhance creativity, not replace it. When used thoughtfully, AI can free up time for more strategic and creative tasks, allowing you to focus on storytelling, brand building, and fostering deeper connections with your audience. The key is to view AI as a collaborator rather than a replacement for human creativity.

There are plenty of real-world examples where AI-assisted content, when balanced with human creativity, has performed exceptionally well. Take **BuzzFeed**, for instance, which uses AI to analyze user data and recommend topics for their viral quizzes. While AI suggests themes based on trends, it's the BuzzFeed team that adds humor, wit, and cultural references that make the quizzes so shareable. This combination of AI data and human creativity ensures that the content resonates on an emotional level, leading to higher engagement.

Similarly, **The New York Times** uses AI to personalize newsletters by recommending articles based on reader preferences. However, the final content is still carefully curated and edited by human journalists who bring nuance, context, and depth to the stories. The AI provides the data-driven foundation, but the human editors ensure the originality and high quality of the content.

Another example is **Sephora**, which utilizes AI-powered chatbots to assist customers with product recommendations based on their preferences and browsing history. While AI handles the technical aspects of matching products to users, the Sephora team ensures that the chatbot's tone and responses align with the brand's friendly and approachable image. This blend of AI-driven efficiency and human touch creates a seamless and enjoyable customer experience.

These examples highlight how AI can significantly enhance the content creation process, but the most successful outcomes always include human input. By combining AI's data-driven insights with your own creativity, originality, and emotional intelligence, you can produce content that not only performs well but also strengthens your connection with your audience. This balance is crucial in maintaining a strong brand presence and ensuring long-term success in social media management.

Chapter 5: Automating Engagement and Analyzing Performance with AI

Tracking engagement and metrics is a vital aspect of social media growth because it provides valuable insights into how your audience interacts with your content and helps you measure the effectiveness of your strategy. Without tracking these metrics, you're essentially operating in the dark, unsure of what works and what doesn't. Engagement metrics, such as likes, shares, comments, and overall reach, offer a clear picture of how your content is resonating with your audience and whether your efforts are driving the desired results.

By understanding how people interact with your posts, you can fine-tune your strategy to focus on the types of content that generate the most engagement. For instance, if you notice that posts with videos are consistently receiving more shares and comments than text-based posts, you can prioritize video content in future campaigns. Similarly, tracking which posts are receiving more likes or comments helps you identify the topics or formats your audience is most interested in, allowing you to create more targeted and engaging content. Without these insights, it's easy to fall into the trap of producing content that doesn't align with your audience's preferences, resulting in lower engagement and reduced visibility on social platforms.

Engagement metrics also play a crucial role in social media algorithms. Platforms like Instagram, Facebook, and Twitter use these metrics to determine which content to promote to a wider audience. Content that receives higher engagement is seen as more valuable and is therefore shown to more users. Tracking your metrics helps you understand which posts are performing well, so you can replicate their success and continue to grow your reach. Additionally, social media growth is closely tied to audience retention and satisfaction, and by tracking engagement metrics, you can ensure that your content is continuously meeting the needs and interests of your followers, preventing them from losing interest or unfollowing your account.

This is where AI becomes a powerful tool for tracking and analyzing engagement. Traditional methods of manually tracking likes, shares, and comments are time-consuming and often prone to human error, especially when managing multiple clients or accounts. AI-driven tools like **Sprout Social**, **Hootsuite**, and **Socialbakers** offer comprehensive solutions for automating the process of tracking engagement metrics. These platforms can collect and analyze large amounts of data in real time, providing you with an instant overview of how your content is performing across all your social media channels.

AI helps you track likes, shares, comments, and overall reach by analyzing patterns in user behavior and engagement. It goes beyond just collecting numbers; AI tools can identify trends in your content performance, such as what time of day posts receive the most interaction or which types of posts are driving the most shares. This allows you to optimize your posting schedule, content format, and messaging to maximize engagement and reach. AI can also provide predictive analytics, showing you which types of posts are likely to perform well in the future based on past data, helping you stay ahead of trends and maintain consistent growth.

One of the key advantages of using AI for engagement tracking is its ability to analyze sentiment. AI tools can sift through comments and interactions to gauge the overall sentiment of your audience, helping you understand how people feel about your content, brand, or products. This level of insight allows you to make adjustments quickly, addressing any negative feedback or amplifying positive responses. For example, if a post about a new product is receiving overwhelmingly positive comments, you can decide to promote it further or create similar content to build on that momentum. On the other hand, if a campaign is receiving negative feedback, AI can flag this early, giving you the opportunity to pivot or address concerns before they escalate.

AI can also segment your audience based on their engagement patterns, allowing you to tailor your content to different groups more effectively. By identifying which segments of your audience are more likely to share your content versus those who primarily comment, you can create targeted campaigns that cater to these behaviors. This personalized approach not only increases engagement but also fosters stronger relationships with your followers, as they feel more connected to your brand when content aligns with their specific interests.

Overall, the combination of engagement tracking and AI analytics provides a powerful way to optimize your social media strategy. Instead of relying on guesswork or manually sifting through data, AI offers an efficient and accurate method of measuring success. By using AI to track engagement metrics such as likes, shares, comments, and overall reach, you can continuously improve your social media presence, ensuring steady growth and a deeper connection with your audience. In a landscape where engagement is the key to visibility and influence, AI gives you the insights and tools needed to stay ahead of the competition and keep your audience engaged and growing.

AI tools like **Sprout Social**, **Hootsuite**, and **Socialbakers** are game-changers when it comes to transforming vast amounts of social media data into actionable insights. These platforms offer advanced analytics that go beyond simple engagement metrics, allowing you to dive deeper into audience behavior, content performance, and overall social media strategy. The key benefit of AI-driven tools is their ability to analyze data in real time, identify trends, and present meaningful patterns that would be difficult, if not impossible, to spot manually.

For instance, **Sprout Social** offers a comprehensive set of AI-powered features that help social media managers and agencies optimize their strategies. It tracks various metrics such as likes, shares, comments, follower growth, and even sentiment analysis, giving you a detailed understanding of how your content is performing. The platform can also analyze posting times and audience activity, helping you determine the best times to publish content to maximize reach and engagement. With AI-driven insights, you can adjust your content strategy on the fly, ensuring that your posts are always optimized for audience interaction.

One of the most valuable features of these tools is their ability to deliver **predictive analytics**. By analyzing past data, AI can forecast how future content might perform, allowing you to plan more effectively. For example, if Sprout Social identifies that posts about a certain product or topic consistently perform well during certain times of the year, you can proactively schedule similar content during those periods to capitalize on audience interest. This type of insight takes the guesswork out of social media management and allows you to make data-driven decisions that lead to better results for your clients.

These AI tools also provide **automated reporting**, which is a huge time-saver. Instead of manually compiling data from different platforms and generating reports for each client, Sprout Social and similar platforms can automate the process. These reports are not just collections of numbers; they offer intelligent insights that explain what's working, what isn't, and where improvements can be made. Automated reporting ensures that you have all the data you need to adjust strategies while also providing your clients with clear, easy-to-understand summaries of their social media performance.

When it comes to using AI analysis to improve client performance and deliver exceptional value, the key is in leveraging these insights strategically. Here are several effective strategies for using AI tools to enhance client outcomes:

1. Optimizing Content Based on Engagement Trends AI tools can analyze which types of content—whether it's videos, infographics, or written posts—perform best with your client's audience. By understanding these trends, you can tailor content strategies to focus on formats that drive the most engagement. For example, if AI analysis reveals that video content outperforms static posts on Instagram, you can allocate more resources to video production, ensuring that your clients are consistently delivering the type of content their audience loves.

2. Targeting the Right Audience Segments One of the most powerful features of AI tools is their ability to segment audiences based on behavior and preferences. Instead of treating your client's followers as one homogeneous group, AI tools can identify different audience segments that respond to specific types of content or interact with posts at certain times. By targeting these segments with personalized content, you can significantly increase engagement rates and ensure that your client's message resonates more deeply with each group. This type of audience segmentation not only boosts performance but also helps clients build stronger relationships with their followers.

3. Timing Posts for Maximum Impact AI tools like Sprout Social analyze historical data to determine the optimal times to post content. Instead of relying on generalized advice or trial and error, AI can pinpoint when your client's specific audience is most active and engaged. This allows you to schedule posts during peak times, ensuring that your content is seen by the largest possible audience. By consistently posting at the right times, you maximize engagement and drive more meaningful interactions for your clients.

4. Enhancing Customer Engagement Through Sentiment Analysis AI tools can also track the sentiment of audience interactions, providing insights into how followers feel about your client's brand or content. Sentiment analysis goes beyond simple engagement metrics by examining the tone and emotional context of comments, mentions, and reviews. If the AI detects negative sentiment in the responses to a particular campaign, you can take proactive measures to address the issue before it escalates. Conversely, if a campaign is receiving overwhelmingly positive feedback, you can double down on similar strategies to keep the momentum going. Sentiment analysis helps you stay in tune with the audience's emotional response, ensuring that your client's brand remains aligned with their followers' preferences and expectations.

5. Improving ROI with AI-Driven Ad Optimization For clients that invest in paid social media advertising, AI tools can significantly improve the return on investment (ROI) by optimizing ad targeting and budgeting. AI can analyze which audience segments are most likely to convert and ensure that your client's ad spend is directed towards those groups. By continuously analyzing ad performance, AI tools can make adjustments in real time, reallocating budget to the highest-performing campaigns. This ensures that your client gets the most value from their ad spend while reducing wasted efforts on underperforming audiences.

6. Refining Long-Term Strategy Through Performance Insights AI-driven analytics offer a long-term view of how your client's social media strategy is evolving. By tracking year-over-year or quarter-over-quarter performance, AI tools can help you identify larger trends and shifts in audience behavior. This allows you to make more informed strategic decisions, such as adjusting your content calendar, diversifying platforms, or experimenting with new types of engagement. The ability to track performance over time ensures that you're not just reacting to short-term trends but also planning for sustained success and growth.

7. Enhancing Client Relationships with Transparent Data Reporting Automated, AI-driven reports provide clients with a clear and comprehensive view of their social media performance. These reports simplify complex data into actionable insights, making it easier for clients to understand the value of your work. By providing transparent, data-backed results, you build trust with your clients and demonstrate your expertise in driving their social media success. Additionally, these reports allow you to set realistic goals with your clients and track progress toward achieving them, ensuring that you're always aligned with their expectations.

By leveraging AI analysis to inform your strategies and decisions, you can dramatically improve the performance of your clients' social media efforts. These tools allow you to optimize content, target the right audiences, improve engagement, and enhance ad performance, all while providing clear, actionable insights that drive results. Ultimately, AI not only enhances the efficiency of your social media management but also enables you to deliver exceptional value to your clients, positioning your business for long-term success.

Chapter 6: Monetizing Your AI-Driven SMM Business

Pricing AI-powered services requires a thoughtful approach, balancing the efficiency AI tools provide with the value of your expertise. While AI can automate many aspects of social media management, your strategic input, creativity, and ability to interpret data are what truly set your services apart. The goal is to ensure your pricing reflects both the time saved through automation and the results delivered, while still maintaining a profitable business model.

Start by considering the costs associated with running your AI-driven social media management business. This includes subscription fees for the AI tools you use, such as scheduling platforms, analytics software, and content creation tools. These costs should factor into your pricing, but you also need to consider the value of your time—whether you're crafting strategies, engaging directly with clients, or interpreting AI-generated data to adjust campaigns.

The key to maintaining profitability is ensuring that your pricing structure isn't based solely on the time saved through AI automation. Instead, clients are paying for the outcomes: increased engagement, improved brand visibility, and the tailored strategies that come from your use of advanced AI tools. By focusing on the value delivered rather than the time spent, you can avoid underpricing your services, even if AI allows you to work more efficiently.

One of the best ways to offer competitive pricing while still maintaining profitability is by creating tiered service packages. This approach allows clients to choose a package that fits their needs and budget, while giving you the opportunity to upsell more advanced services to those looking for greater value. A tiered system also makes it easier to scale your business, as you can offer a range of services that cater to different client expectations.

In a basic package, you might focus primarily on automation, which would appeal to clients who want to maintain an active social media presence without needing complex strategies or in-depth analytics. This package could include services like automated post scheduling, basic AI-generated content creation (such as captions or visuals), and regular performance reports summarizing engagement metrics like likes, comments, and shares. While this package offers minimal manual intervention, it still provides value by ensuring the client's social media presence is consistent and professional. Pricing this package lower reflects the reliance on automation, but it should still account for the strategic setup and oversight you provide.

For clients who need more than just automation, a mid-tier or standard package might offer enhanced engagement tracking and AI-assisted analytics. This package could include everything from the basic level, plus more advanced services such as detailed audience insights, targeted content strategies based on AI data, and personalized consultations to review performance and adjust the social media strategy. At this level, you are offering a blend of automation and human input, using AI to gather data but adding your expertise to fine-tune campaigns. The price of this package should reflect the extra time you spend on strategy, analysis, and consultation, while still leveraging the efficiency AI brings.

For high-end clients seeking a full-service experience, a premium package would offer a comprehensive approach. This package could include everything in the lower tiers, but with deeper engagement such as AI-driven sentiment analysis, audience segmentation, and real-time adjustments based on predictive analytics. Clients in this tier might expect more frequent strategy sessions, advanced performance tracking, and even management of paid ad campaigns using AI to optimize targeting and spend. Pricing for this package should be the highest, as it represents a full investment of your time, expertise, and the advanced capabilities of AI tools. This tier provides the most value, combining automation with high-touch, personalized service that delivers significant results.

By offering these tiered packages, you can cater to different client needs while maximizing value at every level. The basic package appeals to those seeking minimal intervention, while the higher tiers provide more in-depth strategies and personalized services. The key to pricing these packages is ensuring that each tier reflects the combination of AI automation and human expertise, ensuring that you remain profitable even while leveraging technology to streamline your operations.

In summary, competitive pricing for AI-powered services should balance efficiency with value. Offering tiered service packages allows you to meet different client needs while ensuring that you're compensated fairly for both the automation and the strategic input you provide. By focusing on the results your services deliver—whether it's increased engagement, better analytics, or enhanced brand visibility—you can maintain profitability while using AI to improve your workflow and grow your business.

Finding and retaining clients is the cornerstone of any successful business, and leveraging AI-powered marketing tools can significantly enhance your ability to do both. AI provides a competitive edge by allowing you to streamline client acquisition processes, improve targeting, and enhance customer relationships. When combined with the right strategies, these tools not only help you find clients but also enable you to retain them, upsell additional services, and scale your business efficiently without needing to increase your overhead costs.

One of the most effective strategies for finding clients is using AI to analyze and segment potential leads. AI-powered platforms like HubSpot and Zoho CRM use advanced algorithms to identify potential clients based on online behavior, industry trends, and engagement patterns. These tools help you target your ideal audience with precision, ensuring that your marketing efforts are focused on people or businesses who are most likely to benefit from your services. For example, AI can track social media conversations and identify businesses that are actively seeking social media management solutions or struggling to maintain engagement with their audience. This kind of lead generation, which is based on actual data and behavior, is far more efficient than traditional methods of cold outreach.

Once you've identified potential clients, AI tools can assist in crafting personalized marketing messages. Personalization is key in today's business landscape, and AI allows you to tailor your outreach based on specific pain points or needs. For instance, email marketing platforms like Mailchimp or ActiveCampaign use AI to analyze how potential clients interact with previous emails, and then adjust future communications to better resonate with each lead. These tools can automatically send follow-up emails based on engagement triggers, such as when a potential client opens an email or clicks on a particular link. This automated yet personalized approach helps keep your business top of mind for leads, increasing the likelihood of converting them into paying clients.

Retaining clients is equally important, and AI can play a critical role in enhancing the client experience. One of the best ways to ensure client retention is by consistently demonstrating the value you provide. AI tools like Sprout Social or Hootsuite allow you to track your clients' social media performance in real time, generating detailed reports that highlight improvements in engagement, reach, and audience growth. Sharing these insights regularly not only shows the impact of your work but also opens up opportunities to offer additional services based on the data. For example, if the AI tools identify that a particular type of post (such as video content) is performing exceptionally well, you can recommend increasing that type of content or even offer to manage a targeted campaign to capitalize on those insights.

Client retention also involves nurturing relationships, and AI can help streamline this process as well. AI-driven CRM systems like Salesforce use predictive analytics to assess client behavior and forecast their needs. By analyzing engagement patterns, such systems can alert you when a client might be losing interest or when they're ready for an upsell opportunity. This allows you to take proactive steps to engage with the client, offering new strategies or additional services before they even realize they need them. Regular touchpoints, such as personalized emails, performance updates, or strategy meetings, can also be scheduled and automated through AI tools, ensuring that no client is overlooked and that they feel valued throughout their journey with your business.

Upselling additional services is another effective way to grow your business, and AI makes it easier to identify the right opportunities to offer more. By analyzing your clients' social media performance data, AI tools can reveal areas where they could benefit from enhanced services. For example, if your AI reports show that a client's engagement spikes during specific times or on certain platforms, you can recommend expanding their posting schedule or managing paid ad campaigns to take advantage of those high-engagement periods. Similarly, if your AI analytics show that certain content types drive more conversions, you can upsell content creation packages, such as video production or influencer partnerships, to help them achieve even better results.

Scaling your business with minimal overhead is one of the key advantages of using AI. Because AI automates many time-consuming tasks—such as content scheduling, performance tracking, and client reporting—you can manage more clients without needing to hire additional staff. This efficiency allows you to expand your client base while keeping operational costs low. Additionally, AI's ability to provide insights into client performance means you can make data-driven decisions quickly, allowing you to offer high-level services without the need for extensive manual research or analysis. This scalability is essential for businesses that want to grow rapidly but don't want to take on the financial burden of a larger team or increased infrastructure costs.

To further scale your business, you can use AI-powered marketing automation tools to continuously find new leads and convert them into clients. Platforms like HubSpot offer automated lead nurturing sequences that guide potential clients through the buying process, delivering personalized content and offers at the right moments to encourage conversion. These tools allow you to focus on delivering quality service to your existing clients while your lead generation and marketing processes run in the background. As your client base grows, AI tools help you maintain quality and efficiency, ensuring that you can scale your business without sacrificing the personalized service that clients expect.

In summary, AI-powered marketing tools offer powerful solutions for finding and retaining clients while keeping your overhead low. By automating lead generation, personalizing client outreach, and using data-driven insights to upsell services, you can build a sustainable business that scales efficiently. AI allows you to deliver exceptional value to your clients while maximizing your ability to grow, making it an indispensable resource for long-term success.

Chapter 7: Managing Multiple Clients with AI Tools

Managing multiple clients effectively can be a challenging task, especially in a service-driven business like social media management. However, AI offers powerful solutions that allow you to handle various clients simultaneously while maintaining high-quality service. By automating repetitive tasks, AI frees up your time and mental bandwidth, allowing you to focus on the strategic aspects of your business, such as content creation, client relationships, and growth planning. Leveraging AI properly not only increases efficiency but also enhances your ability to scale your operations without compromising service quality.

One of the most effective techniques for juggling multiple clients is centralizing your workflows through AI-powered platforms like **Zoho Social** or **Hootsuite**. These tools allow you to manage multiple social media accounts from a single dashboard, streamlining the entire process. Rather than logging into each platform separately to post content or check performance metrics, AI tools consolidate all your client data in one place. You can easily switch between clients, view upcoming scheduled posts, track real-time engagement, and analyze results, all without needing to manually toggle between different accounts or platforms. This level of centralization ensures that nothing slips through the cracks, and you can efficiently manage multiple clients with minimal effort.

Automating content scheduling is another essential step in managing multiple clients. Tools like **Buffer** or **Later** allow you to plan and schedule posts for weeks or even months in advance. AI-driven platforms can determine the optimal posting times based on audience engagement patterns, ensuring that your clients' content is always published at peak times, even when you're busy working on other projects. Automating these repetitive tasks removes the pressure of having to manually post across various platforms for multiple clients each day. Instead, you can spend time focusing on content strategy, reviewing performance analytics, or brainstorming creative ideas to boost engagement.

AI-powered reporting tools further simplify managing multiple clients by automating the generation of performance reports. Instead of manually pulling data from different social media platforms, AI tools like **Sprout Social** or **Socialbakers** can automatically compile detailed analytics reports. These reports highlight engagement metrics, audience growth, and content performance, making it easier for you to provide value to your clients without spending hours on data collection and analysis. Additionally, automated reports can be customized and scheduled to be sent to clients at regular intervals, ensuring they are kept informed about their social media performance without requiring constant manual input from you.

Another key technique for managing multiple clients effectively is using AI to handle customer engagement and interaction. AI-driven chatbots can be integrated into your clients' social media channels, enabling 24/7 responses to comments, inquiries, and messages. These chatbots can be programmed to provide automated responses to frequently asked questions, share product information, or guide users to specific services. By using AI to automate these interactions, you save significant time and ensure that your clients' audiences receive timely responses, even outside of regular working hours. Chatbots not only keep engagement levels high but also provide a seamless customer experience, which is crucial for maintaining client satisfaction.

Freeing up time for strategy is another critical advantage of AI in managing multiple clients. AI tools can handle the repetitive and time-consuming tasks that typically take up much of your day, such as content scheduling, engagement monitoring, and report generation. With these tasks automated, you can focus on higher-level activities that drive real value for your clients, like developing custom content strategies, running targeted social media campaigns, and analyzing market trends. Instead of spending hours on manual processes, you can dedicate more time to creative brainstorming, data-driven decision-making, and enhancing the overall effectiveness of your clients' social media presence.

For example, AI tools can help you identify the type of content that performs best for each client by analyzing past posts, audience behavior, and engagement trends. This allows you to create more targeted content strategies tailored to each client's audience, ensuring that their social media efforts are always aligned with their business goals. AI can also track real-time social media trends, helping you identify opportunities for your clients to capitalize on popular conversations or viral topics. This level of strategic thinking is where your true value as a social media manager lies, and AI gives you the time and insights needed to focus on these activities.

Another way AI helps streamline operations is by optimizing workflows. With platforms like **Zapier**, you can connect multiple apps and automate workflows across different tools, reducing the need for manual intervention. For example, you can set up workflows that automatically pull new content from a client's website, create social media posts, and schedule them for publication. Similarly, you can automate sending performance reports to clients once a week without needing to manually compile or send them. By automating these workflows, you eliminate repetitive tasks and ensure a consistent, efficient process for each client.

Overall, AI tools provide a significant advantage when it comes to managing multiple clients. By automating repetitive tasks such as content scheduling, engagement tracking, and reporting, you not only increase your efficiency but also free up valuable time for strategy and client management. AI enables you to scale your business while maintaining high-quality service, allowing you to take on more clients without the added stress of managing every detail manually. This balance between automation and strategy is key to growing a successful social media management business and delivering exceptional results to your clients.

To effectively manage client requests, feedback, and performance reports, using the right tools and systems is essential for streamlining communication and maintaining high levels of service, especially as your social media management (SMM) business scales. AI-powered platforms, project management tools, and customer relationship management (CRM) systems play a vital role in helping you manage multiple clients seamlessly, ensuring that nothing is overlooked and that you can maintain a professional, efficient operation.

AI-powered **CRM platforms** like **HubSpot** or **Zoho CRM** are invaluable for managing client relationships. These tools help you centralize client information, track interactions, and store important documents such as contracts, strategies, and reports. AI-enhanced CRMs can automatically log emails, calls, and meeting notes, making it easy to stay on top of ongoing conversations and client requests. Additionally, these platforms provide you with real-time reminders of upcoming deadlines, follow-ups, and milestones, ensuring you stay organized as your client base grows.

Another critical tool for managing client requests and feedback is a **project management platform** like **Trello**, **Asana**, or **Monday.com**. These platforms allow you to create boards or task lists for each client, where you can track the progress of ongoing projects, assign tasks, and communicate with your team in real-time. With AI integrations, these platforms can automatically update task statuses, remind you of pending client requests, or even suggest next steps based on project completion rates. This system of organization keeps everyone on the same page, ensuring that client requests are handled promptly and that projects move forward without unnecessary delays.

For performance reports, AI-driven platforms like **Sprout Social** or **Hootsuite** streamline the process by automating report generation. These tools track key metrics—such as engagement rates, follower growth, and content performance—and compile them into easy-to-understand reports. The reports can be customized to highlight the metrics most relevant to each client, ensuring that you provide data-driven insights in a format that clients can appreciate. These platforms can also automate the delivery of reports, sending them directly to clients at pre-scheduled intervals, allowing you to maintain consistent communication without the manual effort of compiling and emailing each report.

One of the key benefits of AI tools in managing client feedback is the ability to monitor social sentiment in real time. Platforms like **Brandwatch** or **Socialbakers** analyze client mentions and feedback across social media platforms, allowing you to stay informed about what's being said about your clients' brands. This allows for real-time responses and adjustments to strategy based on audience feedback. AI can even identify patterns in client requests or issues, providing insights into common concerns that can be proactively addressed in your strategy updates.

As your SMM business scales, AI tools become even more valuable in maintaining efficiency. Let's look at some **real-world scenarios** of social media management businesses scaling from a handful of clients to managing dozens with the help of AI.

In one example, a boutique SMM agency started with just three small business clients. As the agency grew, they began using **Hootsuite** to automate the scheduling and publishing of social media posts across multiple platforms. By implementing AI-powered tools to handle content scheduling, the team was able to free up time for creative strategy, allowing them to take on new clients without sacrificing the quality of service. In just two years, they scaled to manage over 25 clients, leveraging AI to handle the more repetitive aspects of content management while focusing on personalized strategies and client engagement.

Another example involves an SMM business that specializes in e-commerce brands. Initially, the team managed only five clients manually, but as they started to grow, they adopted **Sprout Social** for performance tracking and reporting. The platform's AI-powered analytics provided deep insights into audience behavior, enabling the agency to refine content strategies for better engagement. By automating performance reports and scheduling, the team expanded to 30 clients within a year, focusing their time on creative campaigns and in-depth strategy sessions while AI handled the bulk of the reporting and scheduling tasks. As a result, they were able to scale without increasing overhead costs or adding significant staff.

Finally, a solo freelancer managing social media for a handful of local businesses began using **Canva** for AI-generated visuals and **Buffer** for post automation. By relying on AI to create professional graphics and schedule posts in advance, the freelancer could onboard more clients while maintaining a lean, one-person operation. As demand grew, the freelancer expanded into a small agency with 15 clients, all managed through AI tools that handled the logistics of content creation and posting. With the bulk of time-consuming tasks automated, the freelancer could focus on strategy and client relationships, allowing for sustainable growth.

These examples highlight how AI tools and systems enable SMM businesses to scale from a few clients to dozens, all while maintaining high-quality service and minimizing overhead. The key to this growth is the automation of repetitive tasks—such as content scheduling, performance tracking, and report generation—which allows businesses to focus on what truly matters: creative strategies and client success. AI ensures that businesses can grow efficiently, taking on more clients without the need for significant increases in staffing or resources, ultimately leading to sustainable, profitable expansion.

Chapter 8: Overcoming Challenges: The Human Touch in an AI-Driven Business

Balancing AI automation with personalized service is key to success because while AI provides efficiency and scalability, it cannot replace the human qualities that build trust, foster relationships, and create a unique brand identity. Clients and their audiences appreciate efficiency, but they also seek connection, creativity, and responsiveness that only humans can provide. By striking the right balance between leveraging AI tools and maintaining a personalized touch, your business can offer the best of both worlds: operational efficiency and meaningful, human-driven service.

AI excels at automating repetitive tasks such as scheduling posts, tracking engagement metrics, and generating reports. This automation frees up time and allows you to manage multiple clients effectively, but relying too heavily on AI without integrating human elements can make your service feel robotic or impersonal. Clients want to know that there is someone behind the scenes who understands their unique needs, goals, and brand voice. While AI can analyze data and suggest optimizations, it lacks the emotional intelligence, creativity, and empathy required to truly connect with clients and their audiences. This is where personalized service comes into play.

Human creativity is one of the most important elements that AI cannot replicate. While AI tools can generate content, analyze performance, or recommend strategies based on data, they are still limited to patterns and historical trends. Creativity, on the other hand, comes from human insights, intuition, and the ability to think outside the box. To infuse your business with creativity, focus on the areas where you can bring new ideas, innovative campaign strategies, and fresh perspectives to your clients. This might involve developing storytelling approaches that resonate emotionally with an audience, creating visually unique content, or coming up with creative solutions to marketing challenges that aren't always rooted in data alone.

Empathy is another critical factor that AI lacks. In any service-based business, clients want to feel heard and understood. AI can assist in tracking client feedback and analyzing sentiment, but it's your ability to empathize with clients, anticipate their needs, and provide thoughtful responses that truly builds long-term relationships. Empathy allows you to adjust your strategies based on a client's evolving goals, business challenges, or personal preferences, ensuring that your service feels customized rather than one-size-fits-all. Whether it's listening carefully to a client's concerns, addressing their frustrations, or celebrating their successes, these human interactions are essential for building trust and loyalty.

Responsiveness is another area where the human touch is invaluable. While AI-powered chatbots or automated emails can handle some aspects of communication, there are times when a client needs a quick, thoughtful response from a real person. Whether it's clarifying a strategy, adjusting a campaign based on performance data, or simply answering a pressing question, your timely and responsive interactions show clients that you are engaged and invested in their success. This level of attentiveness helps you stand out in a crowded market, where many businesses rely too heavily on automation at the expense of personal service.

To infuse your business with human creativity, empathy, and responsiveness, it's important to find ways to integrate these elements into your workflows, even as you rely on AI for efficiency. For example, you can use AI to handle the logistical aspects of your work—like scheduling posts or compiling performance reports—while you focus on creating the actual content and strategy behind those posts. Instead of using AI-generated captions as-is, consider reviewing and tweaking them to match your client's brand voice or adding your personal insights to make them more engaging. This ensures that the output feels unique and tailored to each client, rather than a generic result produced by an algorithm.

When interacting with clients, use AI-powered tools like CRM systems to track communication history, preferences, and client feedback, but always approach each interaction with a personalized, human touch. Take time to understand your clients' long-term goals, the nuances of their brand, and their individual challenges. This approach helps you offer solutions that go beyond the numbers and data, positioning you as a trusted partner rather than just a service provider.

Even in performance reviews and reports, where AI plays a significant role, your ability to interpret the data and provide strategic recommendations makes a big difference. AI can show you what's working and what's not, but your role is to explain why certain strategies are effective, how they align with the client's broader business goals, and what creative changes can be made to further enhance results. This human interpretation adds value to the data, helping clients see the bigger picture and feel more confident in the decisions being made on their behalf.

Ultimately, balancing AI automation with personalized service is what sets successful businesses apart. AI allows you to scale efficiently, manage tasks more effectively, and deliver data-driven insights, but it's the human qualities—creativity, empathy, and responsiveness—that create a lasting impression on clients. By blending both, you can deliver exceptional value, build stronger relationships, and position your business for long-term success in a world where automation alone isn't enough to stand out.

Navigating potential pitfalls such as over-reliance on AI and client dissatisfaction requires a delicate balance between leveraging technology and maintaining human connections. While AI offers incredible benefits in terms of efficiency and data-driven insights, leaning too heavily on it can result in service that feels impersonal, disconnected, or even frustrating to clients. Recognizing the limitations of AI and prioritizing personal interaction is key to avoiding these pitfalls and building strong, lasting client relationships.

One of the most common risks associated with AI over-reliance is the temptation to let automation handle all aspects of client communication and service delivery. For example, while AI-powered tools like chatbots can quickly respond to common queries or provide updates on performance metrics, clients may sometimes feel that their specific concerns are not being addressed. Automation can only go so far, and clients may become dissatisfied if they sense that their unique needs are being handled by generic, automated responses rather than personalized solutions. To avoid this, it's essential to use AI as a tool for enhancing your service, not replacing the personal touch that clients expect.

Another pitfall of over-relying on AI is missing out on the human interpretation and context that is often necessary to make the best strategic decisions. While AI can analyze data and suggest trends or optimizations, it doesn't always account for the nuances that come from understanding the client's business goals, brand values, or audience dynamics. This can lead to recommendations or automated content that may technically be optimized but lacks the deeper connection or creativity needed to truly resonate with the client's audience. AI can crunch the numbers, but only human judgment can take those insights and turn them into meaningful, high-impact strategies.

To mitigate these risks, it's crucial to build strong client relationships that go beyond AI automation. At the core of this approach is regular, meaningful communication. Instead of relying solely on AI-generated reports or automated emails, make it a priority to check in with clients personally, whether through video calls, phone meetings, or tailored emails that go beyond standard updates. Use these touchpoints to not only review performance but also to discuss the broader vision and strategy. This helps clients feel that they're working with a team that understands their unique goals and challenges, rather than just a machine providing data.

Personalized service also plays a key role in building client loyalty. While AI tools can provide excellent insights and efficiencies, clients often remember the moments where you go the extra mile to accommodate their needs or solve a particular problem. This could be offering a quick turnaround on a new campaign, brainstorming creative solutions to a new challenge, or simply taking the time to thoroughly explain why certain strategies are working (or not) based on your interpretation of AI-driven data. These human efforts show clients that you are invested in their success and willing to adapt your approach to meet their specific needs.

Empathy is another critical factor in client retention and satisfaction. AI cannot read between the lines of a client's emotional state or the pressures they may be facing in their business. As you work with clients, listening actively and responding with empathy builds trust and strengthens the relationship. This is especially important when challenges arise. If a client is frustrated with slow progress or feels that their campaign isn't delivering results, a purely AI-driven approach might focus on adjusting metrics or tweaking automation, but a human approach would focus on addressing their concerns, providing reassurance, and working collaboratively to find a solution that aligns with their vision.

It's also important to incorporate a feedback loop into your client relationships. AI tools can gather data on performance, but clients often have feedback on their overall experience that isn't captured by numbers alone. Create opportunities for clients to share how they feel about the process, whether it's through regular review sessions, follow-up emails, or even surveys. This feedback not only helps you refine your services but also shows clients that their input is valued and that they are an integral part of the collaboration. It's this partnership mentality that makes clients feel invested in the process and increases their satisfaction over time.

Building strong client relationships also involves setting realistic expectations and being transparent about how AI fits into the overall service. Clients may have heard about the power of AI and expect instant, flawless results, but it's important to clarify that AI is just one tool in a larger strategy. Setting the right expectations upfront about what AI can and cannot do ensures that clients understand that while AI provides valuable insights and automates repetitive tasks, your expertise and strategic direction are what truly drive success. By positioning AI as an enhancement to your service, rather than the sole driver, you manage client expectations and reduce the risk of dissatisfaction if results don't happen as quickly as they hope.

Ultimately, strong client relationships are built on trust, communication, and a personal commitment to their success. AI can support these efforts by making your work more efficient, providing deeper insights, and helping to streamline operations, but it's the human connection that ensures clients feel understood, valued, and engaged. By blending AI with human interaction—responding empathetically, adapting strategies creatively, and maintaining regular communication—you can deliver a high level of service that not only meets client needs but exceeds their expectations, creating long-term relationships that go beyond the capabilities of automation alone.

Chapter 9: Future Trends: The Evolution of AI in Social Media

Emerging trends in AI are poised to significantly disrupt social media management even further, introducing new capabilities that enhance the way businesses create, distribute, and analyze content. As AI technology continues to evolve, it will bring deeper levels of automation, personalization, and predictive analysis, reshaping how brands engage with their audiences. Staying ahead of these trends will be crucial for AI-driven businesses that want to capitalize on future innovations and maintain a competitive edge in the ever-changing landscape of social media.

One of the most prominent trends is the rise of **AI-generated content** that goes beyond simple text-based automation. While tools like ChatGPT and Jasper.ai already create human-like captions, blog posts, and social media updates, AI is advancing into creating more complex content such as **dynamic videos, 3D visuals**, and even

virtual influencers. These AI-generated influencers are capable of engaging with audiences, participating in branded campaigns, and building a following in the same way human influencers do. Brands that adopt these AI-driven content tools will have the ability to scale content creation without the limitations of human resources, offering them the flexibility to produce more engaging, multi-format content at a rapid pace.

Predictive analytics is another major trend that is set to further disrupt social media management. AI tools are becoming increasingly adept at predicting future trends based on historical data and current user behavior. Platforms like Sprout Social, Hootsuite, and others are incorporating machine learning algorithms that analyze vast amounts of data to forecast which types of content will resonate best with specific audience segments. These AI models can anticipate trending topics, optimal posting times, and even predict shifts in audience behavior before they occur. Social media managers using these predictive insights can craft highly targeted, data-driven strategies that stay ahead of audience preferences, enabling them to adapt quickly and effectively.

Additionally, **AI-powered personalization** is taking engagement to a new level. As AI becomes more sophisticated, it will have the ability to tailor social media experiences on an individual level, delivering content, ads, and messages that are uniquely personalized for each user. This hyper-personalization could include everything from personalized video messages to dynamic content that changes based on a user's past interactions, location, or browsing habits. AI will allow businesses to move away from one-size-fits-all campaigns and instead provide highly relevant, curated experiences for every follower. This shift will lead to higher engagement rates and stronger connections between brands and their audiences.

Social listening and sentiment analysis are also evolving rapidly thanks to AI. While current tools are effective at tracking mentions and analyzing sentiment, future iterations of AI-powered social listening will go even further by understanding context, tone, and even sarcasm. Advanced natural language processing (NLP) algorithms will be able to interpret nuanced online conversations more accurately, helping businesses detect emerging trends, potential PR crises, or new opportunities for engagement. This level of analysis will allow brands to respond to audience sentiment in real-time, ensuring they remain agile and responsive in an increasingly fast-paced digital environment.

As **voice search** and **voice-based interaction** continue to rise, AI's role in social media management will expand to accommodate voice-driven content. Virtual assistants like Alexa, Siri, and Google Assistant are becoming integral to how users search for information and engage with brands. Businesses will need to optimize their social media strategies for voice searches and use AI to develop voice-activated interactions with audiences. This could mean integrating AI chatbots that respond to voice commands or creating content specifically designed to be consumed via voice-activated devices. Staying ahead of this trend will be essential for businesses aiming to capture a growing audience that favors hands-free, voice-driven interactions.

AI-driven businesses that want to stay ahead of the curve and capitalize on these innovations need to remain proactive and forward-thinking. First, it's important to stay informed about the latest developments in AI technology. Regularly exploring new AI tools, attending industry conferences, and participating in online forums or communities centered on AI and social media will help you keep pace with the rapid advancements. Understanding the newest capabilities and trends ensures that your business can adopt cutting-edge tools before competitors, allowing you to differentiate your services and offer more advanced solutions.

Another way to stay ahead is to continually experiment with AI innovations. As new tools and technologies become available, incorporate them into your workflow and test their impact on performance. Whether it's experimenting with AI-generated video content or integrating AI-powered personalization into your campaigns, this trial-and-error approach allows you to discover which innovations drive the most value for your clients. Early adoption not only keeps you ahead of the competition but also positions your business as a thought leader in the industry, attracting clients who are eager to benefit from the latest advancements in AI.

It's also important to focus on **data-driven decision-making** as AI evolves. With predictive analytics and personalized experiences becoming more central to social media strategies, AI-driven businesses must embrace data as a core component of their operations. This means investing in AI tools that can analyze large datasets, predict trends, and offer insights that drive strategy. By making data a key part of how you create content, engage with audiences, and measure success, your business will be better equipped to adapt to the evolving landscape.

Collaboration with AI developers and keeping an eye on future capabilities are also critical for staying ahead. Partnering with AI solution providers, tech startups, or developers who are at the forefront of innovation can give your business early access to tools or features that have not yet become mainstream. Establishing these relationships can also help you provide input on the development of tools that directly address the unique needs of social media management.

Lastly, as AI continues to evolve, it's important to maintain the human aspect of your services. Even as AI becomes more powerful, the need for human creativity, empathy, and strategic thinking will remain crucial. AI can provide the tools and insights, but it's your ability to interpret data, craft unique strategies, and build meaningful client relationships that will keep you competitive. By blending the power of AI with human ingenuity, your business will be well-positioned to capitalize on future innovations while continuing to offer a personalized, high-touch service that clients value.

In summary, the emerging trends in AI—from content generation and predictive analytics to hyper-personalization and social listening—will further disrupt how businesses manage social media. By staying informed, experimenting with new tools, focusing on data-driven decisions, and fostering relationships with AI developers, businesses can stay ahead of the curve and fully capitalize on these innovations. The future of social media management will be shaped by those who can successfully integrate AI advancements while maintaining the human touch that makes their services unique.

Expanding into adjacent areas such as AI-driven digital marketing, e-commerce, and influencer management is a natural evolution for social media management (SMM) businesses looking to diversify their services and capitalize on the growing role of AI in various industries. By branching out into these related fields, you can offer a more comprehensive suite of services that meet the evolving needs of clients while staying ahead of market trends. As AI technology continues to evolve, it's also essential to future-proof your business by being proactive and adaptable to ensure long-term success.

One of the most promising areas for expansion is **AI-driven digital marketing**. Social media is just one part of a brand's broader marketing strategy, and with AI's ability to analyze data and optimize campaigns, you can offer clients services that go beyond social media alone. AI-powered tools like Google Ads and Facebook Ads have already revolutionized paid advertising by optimizing ad targeting, budget allocation, and content delivery in real-time. Expanding into digital marketing allows you to manage paid ad campaigns across platforms, leveraging AI to drive higher ROI for your clients. AI tools can automate audience segmentation, create dynamic ads based on user behavior, and predict which creatives will perform best, giving you a significant edge in managing multi-channel digital marketing strategies.

AI also offers the potential for deeper insights into customer journeys, enabling you to craft personalized marketing funnels that extend beyond social media. By integrating AI with email marketing platforms like Mailchimp or ActiveCampaign, you can develop sophisticated campaigns that nurture leads from initial awareness through to conversion. AI can help optimize these funnels by analyzing which content resonates most with users at each stage, personalizing email sequences based on individual behaviors, and identifying when prospects are most likely to convert. This type of data-driven marketing delivers more value to clients and strengthens their overall digital presence.

E-commerce is another adjacent field that pairs well with AI-driven social media management. As online shopping continues to grow, businesses are increasingly turning to social media as a key channel for driving e-commerce sales. AI tools can play a significant role here by helping brands optimize their social media shops, recommend products to users based on past interactions, and even automate customer service through AI chatbots. For instance, platforms like Shopify and WooCommerce have AI integrations that allow businesses to track customer behavior, offer personalized product recommendations, and automate order management. By expanding your services into e-commerce management, you can offer clients a seamless solution that connects their social media presence with their online storefront, using AI to boost conversions and sales.

Another major opportunity lies in **AI-driven influencer management**. Influencer marketing has become one of the most effective ways for brands to connect with audiences, but managing influencer partnerships can be time-consuming and difficult to scale. AI tools are making it easier to identify relevant influencers, track their performance, and manage campaigns. Platforms like AspireIQ and Traackr use AI to analyze influencer engagement, audience demographics, and content performance, helping brands find the right influencers for their campaigns. By expanding your services to include influencer management, you can offer clients a streamlined way to collaborate with influencers, using AI to monitor campaign success, optimize influencer relationships, and ensure that brand messaging aligns with campaign goals. This not only opens up new revenue streams but also adds a layer of expertise that many businesses find valuable.

As AI continues to evolve, **future-proofing your SMM business** involves being proactive about adopting new technologies and staying flexible in how you deliver services. One way to future-proof your business is by continually educating yourself and your team about the latest AI developments. AI technology is rapidly advancing, and keeping up with emerging tools and innovations ensures that you remain competitive. Attending industry conferences, participating in webinars, and regularly testing new AI tools will help you stay on top of trends and integrate the latest capabilities into your service offerings.

Additionally, investing in AI tools that are scalable and adaptable is critical for staying ahead. The right AI software can grow with your business, allowing you to manage more clients without a corresponding increase in overhead. Look for platforms that offer modular solutions, so as AI continues to develop, you can easily add new features without needing to overhaul your entire system. Whether it's upgrading your CRM with more powerful AI-driven analytics or incorporating new AI tools for personalized content creation, scalability is key to ensuring your business can evolve alongside technological advancements.

Another crucial aspect of future-proofing is diversifying your services. As AI becomes more capable of automating tasks that were previously manual, it's important to expand your value proposition beyond basic social media management. By offering additional services such as digital marketing, e-commerce management, and influencer collaborations, you reduce the risk of becoming too dependent on any one service and broaden your appeal to a wider range of clients. Diversification not only strengthens your business but also positions you as a one-stop solution for clients looking for comprehensive AI-driven strategies.

Fostering strong relationships with AI developers and technology providers can also give your business an edge. As new AI features are rolled out, having access to early versions of these tools can help you experiment with innovations before they become widely available. This early adoption allows you to offer cutting-edge services to your clients, positioning your business as a leader in the field.

Finally, future-proofing means maintaining a balance between AI automation and human input. As AI takes on more tasks, the human touch will remain essential in areas like creative strategy, emotional intelligence, and client relationships. Clients will always value the personal insights and empathy that AI cannot replicate. By blending the efficiency of AI with the unique qualities of human interaction, your business will be better equipped to adapt to the changing landscape while continuing to deliver a high level of service.

In conclusion, expanding into adjacent areas such as AI-driven digital marketing, e-commerce, and influencer management offers exciting opportunities to grow your business and provide more value to clients. Future-proofing your SMM business as AI continues to evolve requires staying informed about new technologies, investing in scalable tools, diversifying your services, and maintaining a balance between automation and human creativity. By staying ahead of the curve and adapting to future trends, you can ensure long-term success in the dynamic world of social media management and beyond.

Conclusion

As we come to the conclusion of this journey into AI-driven social media management, it's clear that the integration of artificial intelligence offers a transformative opportunity for businesses looking to streamline their operations, provide exceptional value to clients, and achieve scalable success. The key takeaways from this book highlight the immense potential AI holds for automating repetitive tasks, delivering data-driven insights, and enhancing personalized engagement, all while allowing social media managers to focus on creativity and strategic growth.

We explored how AI tools can revolutionize core aspects of social media management, from automating post scheduling and content creation to leveraging advanced analytics for more targeted and effective campaigns. AI allows you to manage multiple clients seamlessly, freeing up time for strategy while ensuring that the service you offer remains top-tier. Importantly, we also discussed the balance between automation and human interaction—ensuring that while AI optimizes efficiency, the human touch remains crucial in building strong client relationships, interpreting data, and fostering creativity.

Throughout the book, we've emphasized the importance of staying adaptable as AI continues to evolve. The social media landscape will only become more competitive, and those who embrace AI early will be better positioned to stay ahead of trends and capitalize on emerging technologies. We've outlined strategies for expanding into adjacent areas such as digital marketing, e-commerce, and influencer management, giving you a roadmap for growth and diversification as your business scales.

Now, it's time to take the actionable steps needed to either start or scale your AI-driven social media management business. Begin by assessing your current workflows and identifying where AI can bring immediate efficiency gains—whether it's automating repetitive tasks, refining client communication, or analyzing social media performance. Invest in the right AI tools that align with your business goals, and don't hesitate to experiment with new technologies as they emerge. Build a foundation that integrates AI into your processes but leaves room for the human creativity and strategic thinking that will set your business apart.

Remember, the true power of AI lies in its ability to free you from the constraints of manual tasks, allowing you to focus on the bigger picture—on the creative and strategic initiatives that drive success for your clients and your business. Whether you're just starting out or looking to take your social media management business to the next level, AI can be your most valuable asset in delivering consistent, scalable results while maintaining the personal touch that clients appreciate.

As you move forward, keep in mind that this is an evolving field, and success will come to those who remain curious, adaptable, and forward-thinking. Embrace AI not as a replacement for your skills, but as a powerful tool that enhances your ability to deliver value. The potential for growth and profitability is immense, and by leveraging AI effectively, you can position yourself at the forefront of the social media landscape—ready to seize the opportunities that lie ahead.

With the right blend of AI automation and human ingenuity, the path to success is wide open. Now is the time to take that first step, embrace the power of AI, and build a thriving, future-proof social media management business that delivers results, drives engagement, and scales effortlessly. The future is AI-driven, and with the strategies and insights shared in this book, you are equipped to lead your business into that future with confidence.

www.ingramcontent.com/pod-product-compliance
Lightning Source LLC
LaVergne TN
LVHW051659050326
832903LV00032B/3911